Child Support For The Single Daddy

Understanding Child Support And How
To Avoid Paying Excessive Amounts

Nick Thomas

Copyright © 2015 Nick Thomas

Visit my website at www.singledaddydating.com

ISBN-13: 978-1505405668

ISBN-10: 1505405661

JOIN OUR COMMUNITY!

Single Daddy Dating is a growing community of single fathers who look to help each other, not only with dating success but in all areas of their lives too. This includes parenting, career and finances advice.

Join us today and get '**10 Crucial Checklist To Dating Success For Single Fathers**' completely FREE!

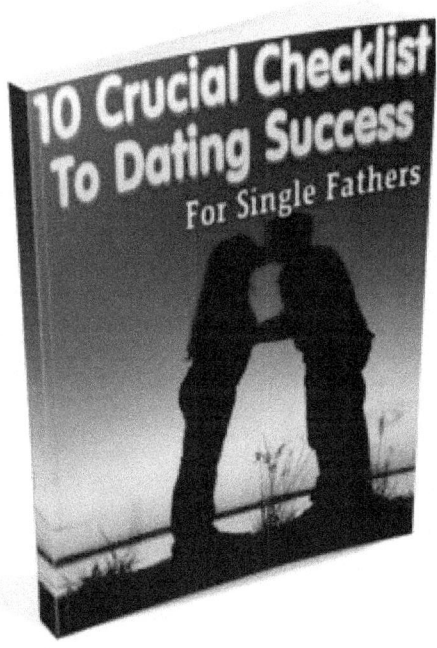

JOIN US AT

CONTENTS

Chapter 1: The Importance Of Child Support

During a divorce proceeding, one of the biggest financial issue that would arise would be child support. Unless you don't have a child from the marriage, child support should be understood thoroughly.

You need to be clear about its importance and how it impacts the children. Besides that, it would also impact the dynamics of the relationship you have with your ex-wife too.

When I was dealing with my divorce, I made it a point to give a high amount of child support. It was partly to ensure that my ex-wife wouldn't need to work too long hours. I didn't want her to worry about money while she was taking care of the children. I want the children to be her main priority.

Luckily for me, I had an understanding and a responsible ex-wife. She cared about the children and understood my intentions. She knew what I wanted to do and appreciated my vision of wanting her to focus on the children. We talked things through, although the marriage was difficult.

In retrospect, I realized how lucky I was that my divorce didn't impact my children terribly. It was to do with the both of us taking the time to mend things and talk things through. We both knew that the marriage was over, but we wanted to ensure that the children would be least impacted.

Other single fathers I know of weren't that lucky. They had terrible divorce proceedings and ended up in tough situations. They were given wrong advice during the divorce proceeding and ended up in great emotional resentment.

All these factors cost them terribly. Over time, they had to deal with the negative effects of divorce. These negative effects not only impacts them emotionally but financially as well.

Child support is the money you pay to support the child. If your ex-wife is the main custodian of the child, it is normal for you to pay her child support to cover the expenses of bringing the child up.

Child support plays an important role in your child's development. Don't treat it like a 'punishment' for needing to pay child support. Rather, treat it like 'child maintenance', so he/she would have the same standard of living and a better future.

When child support isn't consistently given, the child may suffer. If your ex-wife is dependent on that money to buy your child food or other things that your child needs; it would impact the child.

It would also spoil the relationship you have with your ex-wife. The relationship you have with your ex-wife is an important relationship to ensure the successful growth of your child.

Even if both of you are divorced, the two of you still have a relationship – as co-parents. Both of you would need to be in a good relationship because this would help in any discussion you have in the future. You want the relationship to be civil.

According to research, 50.6% of the 13.7 million custodial parents in the US (2009) have some sort of child support agreement in place. Of those agreements, 90% of them were formal agreements established by the courts or government agencies.   9.1% of those agreements meanwhile were informal child support agreements.

The staggering statistic is that 26.8% of custodial parents sought government assistance to collect child support. That amounted to around $35.1 billion in 2009.

This statistic shows that many custodian parents are not getting paid their child support. I hope this isn't you. You need to realize how important child support is to the child.

In this book, I would share about the various issues surrounding child support. Many of these issues have been discussed in our single father support group.

If you are a single father who already been through a divorce, you may be familiar with these issues. Even that, you can still learn about the other potential situations where you need to face, even if you have been divorced.

For other men who are in the midst of a divorce, this book would do you a lot of help. You would understand the basics of doing through a child support process including potential situations you would need to deal with in the future.

Chapter 2: Types Of Child Support

When it comes to child support, there are generally four kinds of child support cases. This is based on the United States legislation.

Many single fathers find it confusing because there are some situations where the child support-paying parent would pay it directly to the custodial-parent while other pay it through the state.

There are generally four kinds of child support cases, namely:-

- **IV-D Cases.** This situation is when the

custodial parent is receiving assistance from the Office Of Child Support Enforcement. These assistance may include establishing paternity, finding the non-custodial parent or establishing and enforcing a child support order.

- **IV-A Cases.** This is a case where the custodial parent receives public assistance from the state. To ensure that the cost of support the family isn't defrayed, the state will refer these cases to the Office Of Child Support Enforcement. This agency helps to collect child support directly from the non-custodial parent.

- **IV-E Cases.** This situation is where the child is being cared for by someone other than the parent. This could be another relative or in a foster care system. These cases are also referred to the Office Of Child Support Enforcement to recoup the costs from the non-custodial parent. In such a case, there is a possibility that both parents are considered 'non-custodial' too. Both of them may need to pay for support too.

- **Non IV-D Cases.** Such cases happen where the child support is established and maintained privately. Some cases would become a 'IV-D Case' when they are referred to the Office Of Child Support Enforcement should there be any outstanding and unpaid child support.

Understanding this various child support cases is important because it highlights the various collection method of child support, together with the potential situations that arise. You need to remember that child support is something that this country has a lot of issues with. You need to understand your responsibilities if you have to pay child support.

Chapter 3: Calculation & Collection

An important aspect of child support is how it is calculated. Different courts in different states apply different formulas to determine child support payments.

There are some courts that don't have a specific formula and rather impose a 'fair amount', according to what it seems fit to the situation.

Besides that, the courts may also have support obligations for a longer period than required by law. It all depends on the state you are in. In this chapter, I would share the basics of the calculation and collection of child support. However, you would still need to take into account the legislation in your own state.

Some main court considerations that would impact the child support calculations include:-

- **Parental Income.** This 'income' may be net or gross. Net being the take-home pay. Besides that, the court may also consider other benefits such as the use of a company car and housing allowance. Should there be any stock valuation, future income increase or lottery winnings, the court would also take them into consideration of the child support calculations.

- **Formula Of Calculation.** Every state has their own formulas, but generally, this is considered of the income of both parents and the number of children. If only one parent is working, then only the income of that parent would be used. The court would also consider other factors such as medical expenses, educational expenses, special-needs children and other recreational activities. All these factor would increase the amount of child support.

- **Cost Of College.** In most states, child support stops when the child reaches the age of majority. This is usually 18 or 21 years old, dependent on the state you are in. However, there are some states which obliges child support for college.

- **Lump Sum vs Per Child.** This is a factor which confuses many single father I know. If a parent is obliged to pay child support until 18 and the obligation covers multiple children, the parent must continue to pay that amount until the youngest child reaches 18 years old. For example if John has child support obligation of $400 for each of his three children and would be on a lump-sum basis, he would need to pay $1200 until his youngest child reaches the age of 18. However, if the support orders specificies that it is an amount per child, the obligation would reduce as each child reaches the age of 18.

To get a clearer idea about such calculations, you would need to visit your state's family court website. It gives a clearer idea about how they specifically use to measure your child support obligation.

When it comes to calculating child support, there are two popular models, the percentage model and the income model.

Some states decide to merge two models in their calculation. Any parent dealing with a divorce would need to understand both these models:-

- **Percentage Model.** In this model, the only income being considered is the non-custodial parent's. The court would calculate child support based on a percentage on his/her income. The percentage would increase as there are more children being considered. Generally, there is a maximum percentage though.

- **Income Model.** In this model, the adjusted income of both the custodial and non-custodial parent is considered in the calculation of child support. From this amount, the court would determine the appropriate child support from each parent based on the parent's share of the support. Then, an amount is calculated to determine the child support obligation. This is a more common model.

There are times where some factors play a role in impacting the amount of child support. The court would deviate from both these models in these situations and use their own methods of calculation.

Chapter 4: How To Prepare For A Child Support Hearing

When attending a child support hearing, there are many men who get afraid. Some of them know that it may amount to a big expense for them if they don't 'perform' well in court. Such thinking is only because they don't understand child support payments and its purpose.

However, I understand their fear that a judge

who knows very little about them and their children would determine the amount of child support needed to be paid.

It should be clear that these judges make the judgments based entirely on the financial information being provided. This system isn't perfect, but the purpose is to protect the children across the country from the effects of divorce.

When preparing for a child support hearing, these are the following things not to do, to get the best out of it:-

- **Don't Have Unrealistic Expectations.** You can't expect to escape from child support payments entirely if your ex-wife doesn't work. Be realistic and argue your way for a more reasonable amount, instead of asking for non-payment. The judge might just get angry at your lack of responsibility and demand that you pay a higher amount instead.

- **Don't Arrive Late.** If you come late, you would create a bad impression of yourself. You don't want the judge to have such an impression of you. Help yourself by arriving early.

- **Don't Fail To Show Up.** This should be common sense. No matter what appointment or activities that you have, the child support hearing should always be a priority. Clear your schedule, your children comes first.

- **Don't Try To Manipulate The Court.** The legal system is about trust. Be totally truthful about every form you fill out and don't miss out on certain information that you are supposed to share. This includes other income that you have. Trying to 'game' the system would only put you in a disadvantaged situation should the judge finds out.

- **Don't Ignore Your Mail.** The court

would send some mail to your lawyer and back to you. You would need to be attentive and not miss any mail. Missing a mail isn't an excuse at all. In fact, when you receive a mail, make sure you read it a few times to ensure that you understand clearly what the court needs.

If you suspect that your ex-wife is trying to mislead the court, you should report the situation to the judge. There are cases where your ex-wife would try to mislead the judge with her income. That's why you should also check the information provided by her.

However, don't be in denial of the situation. Some single fathers don't have their emotions in check and would constantly look to blame their ex-wives for whatever that has happened. Make sure you have your emotions in check first. You want the child support hearing to be as civil as possible.

Chapter 5: Child Support Modification

Child support modification is considered by the courts when there is a substantial change in the child's needs or in the obligor's life. Obligor refers to the child support-paying parent.

There are certain situations in the child's life where his needs changes. Perhaps he has an illness that requires a lot of money to cure or the child has an income source from a work he provides.

There are also other situations where a child suddenly become money-making. He may have a large income, where the child support becomes unnecessary.

A custodial parent can request child support modification is he or she believes that the other parent's income has changed significantly. This can be seen by the lifestyle he lives.

A single father I know of, Barry, had to deal with a similar situation. He was paying meagre child support but his ex-wife found him driving a new sports car.

Because of that, his ex-wife applied to the courts to increase the child support. She was successful with her application after it was found out that Barry had a new job paying him double his previous salary (when the order originated).

There is a possibility that child support

payments would increase when the child's needs increase too. This situations are normally because of unfortunate incidents such as a medical condition.

Besides that, you can also apply for a reduction in child support should there be a significant decrease in your income ever since the child support order was established. These situations can happen when you are retrenched and need to find for another job.

As such, it should be clear that both the custodial and non-custodial parent can apply for child support modifications. However, there are also various factors to consider should you suddenly find yourself in a position where you are unemployed or underemployed.

Considerations For Unemployment

When a custodial parent is going through an

unemployment or underemployment, the courts may decide to institute a search for work order and reserve the child support payment for the future.

For situations where the parent is underemployed, the courts would determine his 'market rate' of his employment and make adjustments. The court would base the child support payments on factors such as work history, education and minimum wage.

The parent would also need to present the following proof of unemployment:-

- Paystubs

- Severance package details

- Termination letters

- Log of job search to match former income level.

These proofs are important because it

determines that the non-custodial parent isn't trying to cheat the system and pay less in child custody payments.

In short, the courts may do the following to calculation the payments of child support by the parent together with other considerations:

- Send an order to the parent to seek for work for a specified period of time. If unsuccessful, the court would order a child support payment based on a minimum level.

- Check to see if the parent has really applied for work from an employer.

- Make reductions on the child support based upon the new employment salary (if successful in finding a new job).

Chapter 6: How Remarriage Changes Child Support

One of the biggest concerns that single fathers have with child support is what happens when either parent remarries.

What would happen if the ex-wife remarries – would the child support change? What would happen if the single father remarries – would the child support change?

A remarriage is perhaps the factor that creates

the biggest change in child support payment. When a custodial parent remarries, the impact isn't that big. Most of the time, the child support would still be maintained and no changes would be made. However, due to other factors, things can still change.

For example, if the custodial parent's new husband has a high standard of living and is known to make good money, the non-custodial parent has the right to argue for a reduction.

Although child support is known as payments by a child's birth parents, the new husband would need to realize that he has responsibilities. These responsibilities might include paying for certain expenses of his step-child.

However, it doesn't mean that you relinquish your parental rights. Most states won't approve a step-parent adoption unless the non-custodial parent has totally relinquish his rights. This rarely happens as you would still want to be a big part of your child's life. You want to make any decisions concerning your child.

Even if your ex-wife (custodial parent) and her new husband are making sufficient income to support your child, you shouldn't elect to totally stop paying child support. There are certain cases where the ex-wife elects to stop receiving child support. This isn't advisable.

As a single father, you still want to play an important role in your child's life. Even if the money is sufficient for the child's day-to-day expenses, you can put the money into a Section 529 plan for his future college needs.

Many single fathers also have concerns about what would happen if he remarries. If a single father remarries, the important thing to know is that the income of his new wife wouldn't be considered in any child support modification.

However, things can be different should you have another child with your new wife. There are states that allow modifications in such situations. This means that you can apply for a lower child support for your child (in the previous marriage).

Most courts however, are reluctant to reduce child support on these grounds. You would need to provide a strong case that your child (from the previous marriage) can still 'survive' and that your ex-wife can still cope with a reduced child support payment.

In general, a remarriage rarely changes a child support agreement. However, it would create some knock-on effects that allows you to argue for a reduction in child support payments.

You need to see if your child's life would be impacted if you reduce child support. Although you are paying the money to your ex-wife, the purpose of child support is for your child.

Speak to a lawyer about your situation to see what he advises you to do. Every situation is different.

Chapter 7: Government Assistance & Child Support

Government assistance can be something that many single fathers are looking for, as they have problem coping financially. Paying child support is difficult because it would take away a chunk of money each month. For this matter, government benefits may be granted.

Before you are granted any benefits, the government office would first inquire as to whether you have been paying child support. If not, the government would make every effort to collect child support from you, to recoup some expenses that would otherwise be paid for by the government.

However, many single fathers have difficulties applying for public aid when a child support order is in place, because government support is based on income. If approved, the benefits may include food stamps, day care, financial assistance and housing assistance.

Before government benefits are approved, you would need an actual divorce order in place. Single fathers who are seeking government assistance and has yet to divorce should seek a legal separation agreement filed with the court, before they apply for government assistance.

The state would always prefer that the child receive child support instead of public assistance. That is the rule for single fathers wanting to apply for government assistance. To qualify for government assistance, you would have to file for child support first. This is because the government believes that both parents should be providing financial assistance before the government steps in to provide additional financial help.

Therefore, if a single mother who isn't receiving child support requests for public assistance on behalf of the child, the state would initiate a child support case first.

It doesn't matter if the mother wants a child support case filed or not. Therefore, you need to realize this as a single father. If your ex-wife filed for government assistance, you would most probably be affected.

There are some single fathers who wonder whether if they would receive more money by filing for child support or by government assistance. Single fathers need to think about the following:

- Public assistance may reduce or cancel your case if it has been found out that child support funds are sufficient to support the child.

- A parent may decide to stop child's government assistance case if he/she determines that the child support funds are sufficient.

- Even without public assistance funds, the parent may still receive other form of assistance for a child such as food stamps and medical benefits.

In many states, a single parent can't receive both child support and public assistance. Your ex-wife need to be aware of this. As a single father, understanding government assistance is an important part because if your ex-wife applies for public assistance, it may raise a child support order.

However, it should be noted that the law

surrounding child support and public assistance is complicated. Added to the complexity of each case, it makes it even more difficult. For more detailed and specific information, you would need the advice of a family law lawyer.

Chapter 8:
Deadbeat Parents

Deadbeat parents are parents who are obliged to pay for child support but have fallen behind those payments. In fact, there is even an act for it, called the Deadbeat Parents Punishment Act of 1989. This act defines deadbeat as someone who chooses not to pay child support. It is considered a wilful act.

I can understand that many parents find it difficult to fulfil their child support obligation during a difficult. There are many things that can happen such as a loss of job, disability or income reduction. However, these aren't considered 'deadbeat'.

Just because you fall behind on child support payments doesn't make you a 'deadbeat' parent. A true 'deadbeat' is someone who can make those payments but choose not to.

There are many individuals who are employed and can easily pay for the child support but don't pay. Instead, they spend their money on other things like on a new partner, car or even their own housing. These are selfish individuals who have no regard for their children, and the law.

We like to stereotype situations, but deadbeat parents aren't only fathers. There are many mothers who are obliged to pay for child support but simply refuses to do so.

According to the Deadbeat Parent Punishment Act (DPPA) a parent who falls behind payments once or twice wouldn't need to face charges. Federal prosecution only comes when the parent have wilfully failed to pay child support for more than twelve month or owe more than $5,000 in unpaid support.

Even in my single father experience, I have known many deadbeat fathers. I'm not saying that all deadbeat parents are fathers, but they are simply who I meet.

I have met many deadbeat fathers who express their total disregard about paying child support. Many of them think that child support is simply paying money to their ex-wives.

I get angry whenever I talk to them. I try to explain to them that child support isn't to pay the ex-wife, but for the ex-wife to support the children.

Many of them remain indignant though. They are adamant that they shouldn't have to pay for child support. Over the years, I have hoped that these people would get punished in the future.

Fortunately, I have seen many of them being punished (as mean as it sounds). Many of them have court orders sent to them and their ex-wives creating plenty of troubles for them. I have seen ex-wives shaming them and making their lives miserable. I have also seen their children not wanting to be with them.

This is all because of their wrong misconception of child support. Never treat child support like a small matter. Treating child support as a small matter is like thinking that you don't have to bring up a biological child that treats you as a father. It is simply irresponsible.

Chapter 9: Tom Romney

Tom Romney has told me a lot about his life as a single father. He was struggling to make ends meet after the divorce. Things was difficult after he had to pay a great deal of alimony and child support. His ex-wife was a blood-sucking woman who had no mercy on him.

In the back of his head, he didn't mind paying that much money to her if it meant that his children get well taken care of. Only problem was, they weren't. His ex-wife was a spendthrift who didn't know how to budget.

She would buy luxuries without caring about the future. That was the main reason why they eventually got a divorce.

They had joint custody of the children but struggled to co-parent them together. The ex-wife was a tough woman to deal with, especially after the divorce. She would try to make life difficult for him in all situations – constantly looking to get more money from him and over time, his life became miserable.

Tom came to me because he wanted to pay less alimony and child support to her. He felt that she didn't need so much money. She wasn't managing the money well and it only taught his two children a bad example of financial management.

I talked to him and he seem pretty adamant on trying to modify his child support and alimony. But, he didn't considered other alternative.

He went to a lawyer and the lawyer advised him to modify his alimony payments instead of the child support. The lawyer told him that he would be able to save on alimony because the ex-wife should be capable of working. Saving on child support on the other hand, can be detrimental on the children.

Tom didn't want his children's lifestyle to take a hit. He knew that his two children are active children who have tons of activities. He want them to continue all those activities – things like soccer, class trips etc.

Tom managed to bring the proceeding to court and reduced his alimony. He also managed to modify his child support payments.

He would give a certain amount to his ex-wife but she would need to prove on the amounts spent on the child. This means that any payment records made for the children would need to be kept.

Tom proved to the court that his ex-wife was a spendthrift and the court didn't want her to spend unnecessarily. It was something that Tom was happy about.

From there on, Tom managed to create a better financial future for himself and his children. He has set up a 529 plan for his children and look to send his children to college in the future. His ex-wife on the other hand has started working again, making more money to support her children.

In the past year, Tom has met a wonderful woman. She is an amazing and beautiful woman that Tom deeply adores. Even his children loves her. He has never been happier after the divorce.

Tom's story goes to show that child support modification doesn't need to be only on the amount of money being paid. You have to understand the various changes that can be made too. Your situation may be different from the situation other single fathers face, but changes can still be made.

Talk to a trusted divorce lawyer and see what he/she advises. Tell him/her about your situation and be clear about what you want.

Final Notes

The issue of child support often get single fathers into plenty of confusion. The idea of child support seems great – supporting the child financially. However, does the money really help the child/children?

It has to be said however that there are many single fathers out there who are defaulting on their child support payments. The situation has been getting worst in recent years.

The reasons for this are many, but the main factor has to be the excessive amount of child support single fathers need to pay in the first place.

In my single father support group, most of them are responsible men. If you come to support groups looking to be a better parent, you would most probably be a responsible person. It has to be said that most of them DO pay too much in child support without realizing.

Therefore, you need to think about the various issues concerning child support to know what you can do. Having a proper child support in place ensures ease in your life. You can build a better life for yourself and children.

This book isn't the be-all of child support. You won't be able to understand everything about child support from this short book. My intention for this book isn't to give you a thorough understanding of child support. Rather, it is to give you a clearer understanding about what to expect.

There are many possibilities when it comes to

child support that many single fathers are completely unaware of. Therein lies the power of being in a single father support group. You get to hear stories and advise from other single fathers. Many of their experience are even more valuable than professionals such as lawyers or therapist.

As a fellow single father, I wish you luck. Always be learning, it would help you over the long run.

LEAVE A REVIEW

I hope this book has helped you well. It isn't my intention at all to go deep into the topic. I am no expert in everything. However, I have the help of many other single fathers who have shared with me their invaluable experience.

If this book has helped you in any way, do leave me a review. This helps build our single father community.

If you feel that this book can be improved in any way, do mention it in the review. I would love to hear from you.

I wish you luck as a single father…

ABOUT NICK THOMAS

Nicholas Thomas has helped many single fathers cope with divorce in the past few years. By helping them gain more confidence and stability in their lives, he is able to guide them towards being a man that attracts other women easily.

He divorced back in 2008 and knows how difficult a divorce can be for a man. It was a terrible time for him when he got his divorce. He envisioned his children blaming him and not being able to spend time with him. It gave him a constant guilt trip.

Being a divorced man can be very difficult. Ever since his 'emotional recovery' from the divorce, he has helped many single fathers by advising and helping them gain confidence.

Should you want to share your story with him, you can do so at
www.singledaddydating.com/shareastory/

ALSO BY NICK THOMAS

(1) Dating After Divorce For The Single Daddy

(2) Dating Ideas For The Single Daddy

(3) How To Be An Alpha Male

(4) First Date Conversations

(5) Online Dating

(6) How To Approach Women

(7) Mature Dating

(8) Single Parent Support

(9) Coping With Divorce

(10) Parenting After Divorce

Visit www.singledaddydating.com/bookstore/

Get Your Complimentary
FREE BOOK

Join our community today and get **10 Crucial Checklist To Dating Success For Single Fathers** FREE, delivered right to your email…

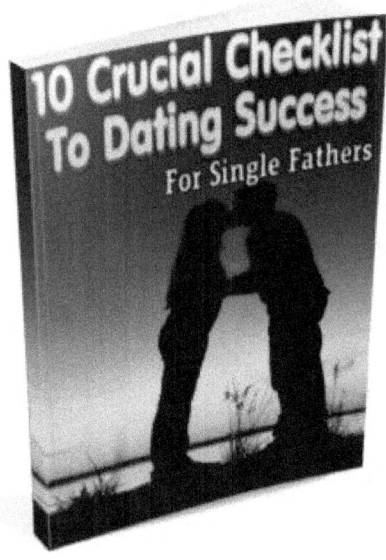

JOIN US AT
**WWW.SINGLEDADDYDATING.COM/
NEWSLETTER/**